GERMAN LIGHT RECONNAISSANCE VEHICLES

A light armored scout vehicle, Sd.Kfz. 222, in the Ukraine. The two boxes on the left front fender are of particular interest (as is the horse-shoe, a good luck symbol), and on the nose, the steel helmets ahead of the lights, the cover on the spare wheel and the dust covers on the mouths of the weapons. (BA)

HORST SCHEIBERT

Schiffer Military/Aviation History
Atglen, PA

PHOTO CREDITS

Federal Archives, Koblenz (BA)
Munin Publishers (M)
Guderian Archives
Schroeder Archives
Hintze Archives
Podzun Archives
Military History Research Agengy, Freiburg (MGFA)
TAMIYA (color pictures)

Translated from the German by Edward Force.

This book originally appeared under the title,
Deutsche Liechte Panzerspähwagen,
by Podzun-Pallas Verlag, Friedberg.

Copyright © 1993 by Schiffer Publishing Ltd.

Printed in the United States of America.
ISBN: 0-88740-522-3

We are interested in hearing from authors with book ideas on related topics.

Published by Schiffer Publishing Ltd.
77 Lower Valley Road
Atglen, PA 19310
Please write for a free catalog.
This book may be purchased from the publisher.
Please include $2.95 postage.
Try your bookstore first.

This is also a Sd.Kfz. 222 – seen here with winter paint, a cover over the grid flaps on top, a wire screen in front of the headlights, a protective frame around the Nottek light on the fender, and towing cables already in place.

Light Armored Scout Vehicles, 1932 to 1945

The Treaty of Versailles banned the German Reich from building armored vehicles on tracks; only armored wheeled vehicles were permitted, and the Reichswehr had several examples of various kinds. Two-axle (four-wheel) chassis were planned as light versions for future construction.

The only really useful vehicles, though, were the small armored vehicles first built in 1932. There were two versions:

Kfz. 13 (Machine-gun Vehicle) with Dreyse 13 machine gun and two-man crew.

Kfz. 14 (Radio Vehicle) with no armament, only radio equipment and three-man crew.

These first, purposefully developed vehicles on wheels were only a makeshift solution, built for the troops until 1935. They existed in several versions:

Sd.Kfz. 221 (Light Armored Scout Vehicle) with MG 34 (later MG 42) and two-man crew.

Sd.Kfz. 221 (Light Armored Scout Vehicle) with a 2.8 cm antitank gun and two-man crew.

Sd.Kfz. 222 (Light Armored Scout Vehicle) with 2 cm KwK and on 3 MG 34 (later 42) and three-man crew.

Sd.Kfz. 222 (Light Armored Scout Vehicle) with the same armament, plus a hanging gun mount for better anti-aircraft defense.

Sd.Kfz. 223 (Light Armored Scout Vehicle) with radio equipment and one MG 34 (later 42) and three-man crew.

Sd.Kfz. 260 (Small Armored Radio Vehicle), unarmed, with four-man crew.

Sd.Kfz. 261 (Small Armored Radio Vehicle) with frame antenna, (later) one MG 42 behind a shield, and four-man crew.

There were also several command vehicles, but they were based on other chassis and motors:

Sd.Kfz. 247 Type A, unarmed, with only radio equipment.

Sd.Kfz. 247 Type B, unarmed, with radio equipment and crew up to six men.

As of 1943, a halftrack vehicle, a Light Scout vehicle, was supplied to the troops as a basic armed and armored vehicle:

Sd.Kfz. 250/9 "Caesar" with one 2 cm KwK and one MG 34; three-man crew.

Finally, there was a full-track light armored scout vehicle with the chassis of the Panzer II tank, Type L:

Sd.Kfz. 123 "Lynx" with one 2 cm KwK and one MG 34, three-man crew.

To equip entire units of the Wehrmacht, Waffen-SS and Police, there was also the light French Panhard 178-P 204 (f) light armored scout vehicle, taken over from the Czech Army in 1939 and captured in great numbers during the French campaign in 1940.

Other light scout vehicles that saw service for Germany were captured vehicles that were taken individually or in small numbers by the troops at the front and – as long as spare parts and ammunition were available – put to use. They usually had only a short life and are not shown here.

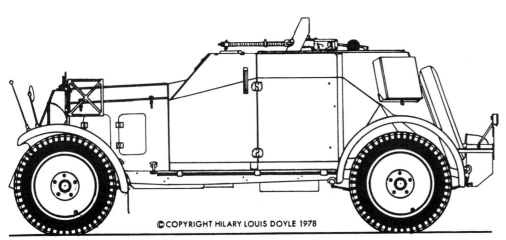

Above: During peacetime maneuvers.

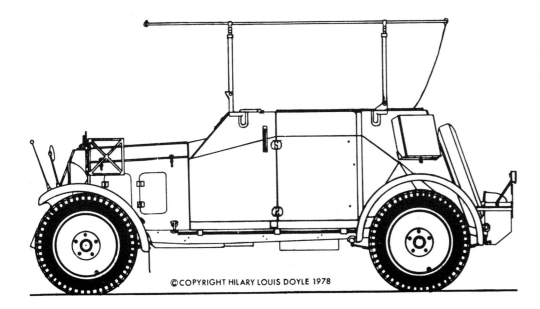

Left: Drawings of the machine-gun vehicle, Kfz. 13 (above), and the radio vehicle, Kfz. 14.

They were only lightly armored, and both bore the nickname of "bathtub." Despite their weaknesses, they saw service until 1941, usually with the reconnaissance units of infantry divisions.

Small Armored Motor Vehicles

The first small German armored vehicles were Kfz. 13 and 14. They were based on the chassis of the "Standard 6" type built at the Adler Works in Frankfurt. Their armored superstructures of 8 mm sheet iron were made by the Deutsche Edelstahl AG in Hannover but were not secure against SmK fire. Production began in 1932 and ended in 1934. In all, 147 of the Kfz. 13 or Kfz. 14 were built.

While the Kfz. 13 Machine Gun Vehicle was armed with a Dreyse 13 machine gun behind a protective shield, the Kfz. 14 Radio Vehicle carried no armament. Instead it carried radio equipment, as indicated by its larger crew of three men. It had a frame antenna that could be folded down. The off-road capability of these vehicles was limited – particularly because of their high center of gravity.

Until the introduction of the successor model (Light Armored Scout Vehicle), they saw service in the cavalry and reconnaissance units of the Reichswehr and Wehrmacht. Individual specimens still saw service until 1941. These vehicles, open on top, were nicknamed "bathtubs" by the troops.

Right: these two pictures clearly show the differences between Kfz. 13 (above) and Kfz. 14. They were also designated "Medium Armored Passenger Vehicle Adler."

Upper left: A Kfz. 14 with half-erected frame antenna, seen during prewar training.

Above: This vehicle was also photographed before the war. The Panzer troop uniforms of the crew (seldom seen in connection with this vehicle) indicate that this vehicle belonged to the reconnaissance unit (motorized) of a Panzer division.

Above and upper right: These two photos show action during the Polish campaign. Of particular interest is the varying way of applying the white cross to the sides of the vehicles; above, it is right in the middle of the side armor, at upper right, farther forward at the driver's level – and this vehicle has a name painted on the vertical side armor. The tactical symbol indicates a reconnaissance unit.

Right: This picture shows action in the French campaign. The Kfz. 13, seen here along with a Sd.Kfz. 223, bears the (rare) German cross, customary as of 1940, as a sign of recognition or a national emblem.

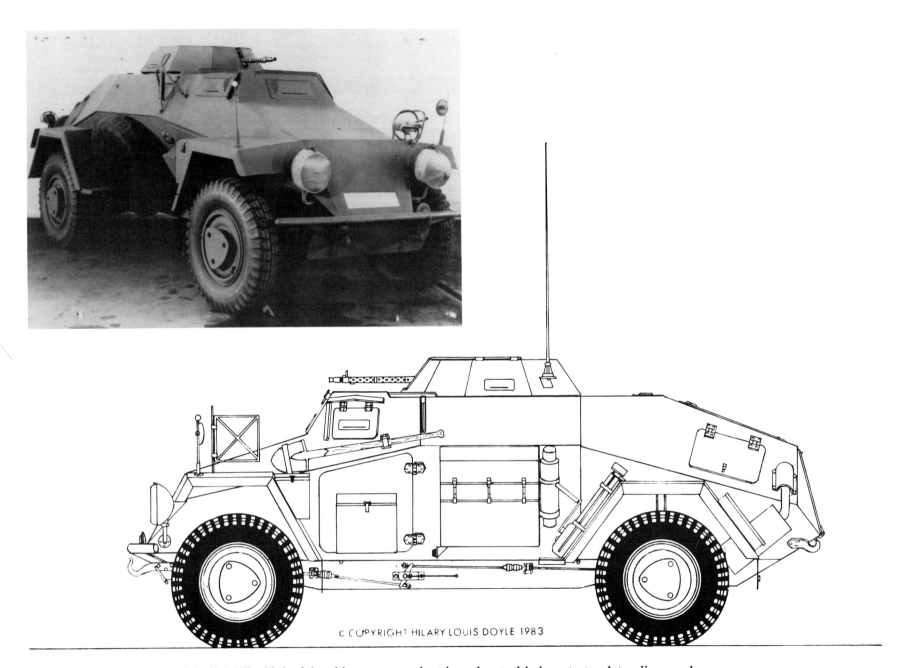

C COPYRIGHT HILARY LOUIS DOYLE 1983

A light armored scout vehicle (Sd. Kfz. 221) of the older type –not the triangular steel-hub protector, later dispensed with. (MGFA)

Light Armored Scout Vehicle, Sd. Kfz. 221

The first really useful light armored vehicle made in Germany was the Special Vehicle 221. It was developed at the Eisenwerk Weserhütte AG in Bad Oeynhausen and assembled by two firms, Schichau in Elbing and the Maschinenfabrik Niedersachsen in Hannover (MNH), from 1935 to 1940. The chassis was built in Zwickau by Horch and called Einheitsfahrgestell (Uniform Chassis) 1 (801) for heavy (armored) motor vehicles. The motor was also built by the Horch branch of the Auto Union AG.

It differed from its slightly bigger counterpart, Sd.Kfz. 222 (and 223), which was built at the same time, in having a single large driver's window (222 and 223 had two smaller ones), a smoothly descending tail design (the 222 and 223 had a step just below the turret), a rectangular radiator at the rear (unlike the trapezoid-shaped type of the 222), and a crew of only two men.

Along with the pure machine-gun vehicle – originally armed with the MG 34, later the MG 42 – there were a few individual vehicles armed with the 2.8 cm Panzerbüchse 39, later 41, behind a flat shield and mounted in a somewhat modified turret. A wire screen could be folded over its turret, which was open at the top, for protection against hand grenades.

With a 75 HP motor mounted in the rear, it was somewhat underpowered for its weight of four tons. Its four-wheel drive (which could be shifted to two-wheel drive for road use) gave it satisfactory off-road capability. All in all, the

vehicle was rather complex and thus often needed repairs. 339 of these vehicles were built.

All the armored reconnaissance units then existing in the armored, light and infantry divisions (motorized) were equipped with them.

A photo taken during the union with Austria in 1938 – here the Reconnaissance Unit (motorized) 2 of the 2nd Panzer Division marches through Vienna. In front are three Sd.Kfz. 221 vehicles, in back is a 222.

Below: The angled rear body becomes the upper engine cover without a step (this shows the 222).

Upper left: One of the two prototypes of Sd.Kfz. 221. The raised area over the driver, visible here, was eliminated in the later production vehicles. It shows the rigid pennant customary in peacetime. To it, coverings of red or blue cloth were attached to show which side it was on in training. The triangular pieces of armor plate to protect the wheel bearings are also easy to see here; they were eliminated later.

Above: This Sd.Kfz. 221 was sold to the Chinese army. Its machine gun was taken out of its usual position so that it could be aimed more vertically for defense against aircraft. The square rear grille is almost always an identifying mark of the 221 (though a few early 223 vehicles also had it).

All three photos on this page show – as the white cross makes clear – action in the campaign against Poland. The crosses on the noses are of particular interest. They were intended to provide instant recognition when troops met. But as they also provided good targets, they were eliminated later.

As can be seen in the lower photo, the driver's lookout could be opened all the way, uncovering a transparent window that kept dust out.

Upper left: The bundle of logs attached to the front could provide help in rough country. The machine gun has been covered by a tarpaulin.

Above: Note the two canisters on the front fenders and the cover stowed on the nose. The towing cable is already in place, so as to lose no time in an emergency. (M)

Left: For protection against hand grenades, the open turret could be covered by folding screens. The storage cases on the front fender and on the sides of the hull are easy to see, as is a fire extinguisher. (BA)

Ukraine, winter of 1941-42. Beside the machine gun, a captured Russian antitank gun can be recognized. Here too, the towing cable is already in place, and an ammunition box has been attached to the bow for additional storage space. In the steppes of Russia, these vehicles often served as observation points.

Above: In North Africa too – here at Hill 102, 22 kilometers west of El Gazala – the 221 served as an observation platform. Note the antenna of this vehicle. This equipment was added later, from 1941 on. It did not exist in the French campaign. (BA)

Left: A 221 stands guard along the channel coast of France.

A few Sd.Kfz. 221 vehicles were also built with a 2.8 cm antitank gun. For this the turret had to be cut away somewhat in front.

In the upper right photo, there seems to be such a weapon under the tarpaulin. This vehicle also has a staff antenna. The photo was taken during Operation "Citadel" in 1943. (BA)

The 221 in the photo at right shows both a machine gun and a Russian antitank gun under the tarpaulin. In addition to the swastika flag for identification from the air, this vehicle also has an antenna. (BA)

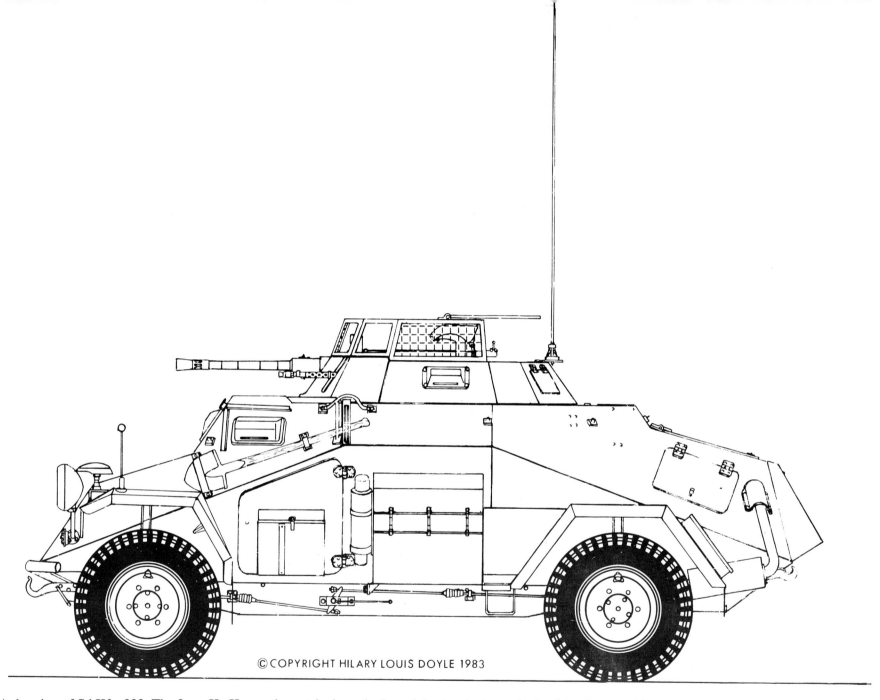

A drawing of Sd.Kfz. 222. The 2 cm KwK gun, the notched rear body and the two lookouts in the driver's area differenti-
ate it from the 221.

Light Armored Scout Vehicle, Sd.Kfz. 222 and 223

Almost simultaneously, having been planned to complement the Sd.Kfz. 221, 989 Type 222 light armored scout vehicles were built from 1936 to 1943 and 550 Type 223 light armored scout vehicles from 1935 to 1944. They were built to designs made by the Weserhütte AG at the Schichau works in Elbing and the MNH and Büssing-NAG factories.

Each type carried a three-man crew. While the 222 was more heavily armed (one 2 cm KwK and one MG 34, later MG 42) than the 221, the 223 was purely a radio vehicle. It was therefore also called the Standard Armored Radio Vehicle. It carried only one machine gun for self-defense. Its frame antenna, along with the FuG 19 SE 30 (later FuG 12), allowed it to cover large distances by radio.

Its chassis (Uniform Chassis II by Horch/Auto Union for heavy armored passenger vehicles) and its motor (likewise by Horch) were somewhat larger and stronger (81 HP, later 90 HP) than those of the 221. Later versions had a lengthened tail with an air filter attached in front of the radiator, a hanging mount for weapons to provide better anti-aircraft defense (troop air protection), while lacking the triangular wheel-bearing armor and somewhat higher folding screen over the turret opening. The hanging gun mount was sometimes installed in earlier versions as well. Light reconnaissance units usually had one 221 and one 223, or one 222 and one 223. All three vehicles (221, 222 and 223), including also the Armored Radio Vehicles 260 and 261, were also called

"Horch Wagons" by the troops. While the 221 could reach a top speed of 90 kph, the 222 and 223 could attain only 85 kph – limited mainly by their higher weight (4.8 and 4.4 tons respectively), compared to only two tons for the 221.

There were two types of the Sd.Kfz. 222. The earlier (at left) has lower turret screens, two lookouts of equal size ahead of the driver, an unprotected grille to the rear, and no handholds near the side lookouts.

Upper left: An older-type vehicle, recognizable by its wheel hubs. Note that the weapons are mounted very low. (MGFA)

Above and left: As of 1940, hanging mounts were installed – to some older models as well – for better anti-aircraft defense. In the picture above, one is seen on a later-type vehicle (with different-sized front lookouts). In the photo at left, taken in Africa, a later type can also be recognized by the handholds on the sides. (1 x BA)

The photos on this page show the 222 in action in Poland. They naturally show the earlier version. In the picture at right, the 222 can be recognized by the two crewmen in the turret (the 221 had only one) and the step at the rear. The scout vehicle of Reconnaissance Regiment 9, at upper right, hit a mine. (1 x BA)

An older type (note the equally large lookouts in the driver's area, the wheel-hub protectors and the lack of handholds on the side armor) shot down in the French campaign (1940), but already showing a hanging mount for a 2 cm machine gun. (BA)

Above: The hanging mount (also installed in an earlier type here) is easy to recognize. (BA)

Upper right: A 222 in a French city in 1940. (BA)

Right: A 222 of the 20th Panzer Division in southern Russia in 1942. The different-size lookouts indicate that it is a later version.

Upper left: The license plates of these two Sd.Kfz. (a later 222 in front, a 223 behind in) of the 24th Panzer Division are of special interest. The letters and numbers were painted in white on a black background!

Above: A 222 of an SS cavalry division without a 2 cm gun. This is an early version – but already has handholds on the sides.

Left: The later type (with high turret screens) of an SS unit (Balkan campaign, 1941).

All three photos were taken during the North African campaign and show later types – since only these versions generally saw action there – with dust filters for their rear grilles. They were later attached in other theaters of war as well, lengthening the vehicles noticeably.

Above: Unloading in Tripoli, 1941.

Upper right: This picture shows a 221 at left and a Sd.Kfz. 251 in the center (1942). (2 x BA)

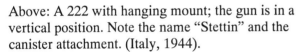

Above: A 222 with hanging mount; the gun is in a vertical position. Note the name "Stettin" and the canister attachment. (Italy, 1944).

Upper right: a newer-type 222 with high turret screens (here covered by a tarpaulin).

Right: This photo, taken in 1944 (19th Panzer Division), shows that earlier versions (wheel-hub protectors, no air filter) were still in service at that time.

Opposite page: This 222 also carries a lot of baggage (they were nicknamed "gypsy caravans" in those days). It is ready to be loaded into an open Me 323 plane. (BA)

Upper left: Africa, 1941: four Sd.Kfz. 222 and one eight-wheel engineer scout vehicle. (BA)

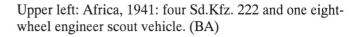

Above: This 222 bears two African palm tree symbols and the name "Siegfried." (BA)

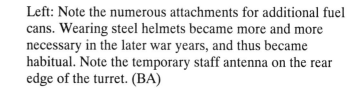

Left: Note the numerous attachments for additional fuel cans. Wearing steel helmets became more and more necessary in the later war years, and thus became habitual. Note the temporary staff antenna on the rear edge of the turret. (BA)

On these two pages we see the Sd.Kfz. 223 armored radio vehicle. It was generally based on the earlier chassis of the 222, it had a turret armed only with a machine gun, and is identifiable by its folding frame antenna.

On the next page we see a 223 on parade in Berlin before the war (upper left), and in Russia in 1941 (here with a later-type chassis and dissimilar front lookouts), at lower left in Poland, and beside it a version with only one driver's lookout (a rarity!). (1 x BA)

A 223 (in back) and a 221 seen during the Polish campaign. They have no screen over the open turret top, and no handholds on the sides. The berets of the Panzer troops, made with strong rubber padding inside (which present-day Bundeswehr berets lack), were worn only until 1941. They also made good pillows.

This 223, seen during a battle in a Russian town, has screens that fold outward. As can be seen in other pictures in this book, there were also screens that folded up and in against each other. The 223 had a different turret from the similar Sd.Kfz. 261.

Upper left: A 222 (left) and a 223 side by side during the French campaign (1940). Both have wire screens on the rear. The combination of the two types for joint action was common.

Above: This armored radio vehicle of the communications battalion of the 5th Panzer Division shows the typical 222 rear end, which proves that it is a 223. The similar 261 usually had the square rear of the 221 and, above all, no turret. Here the wire screens generally fold inward.

Left: Here too, a 222 and a 223 of the SS Panzer Division "Leibstandarte Adolf Hitler" (LAH) stand side by side (Balkan campaign, 1941). The different turret sizes are easy to see. (M)

Above: A Luftwaffe 223 seen during the French campaign. It served the aircraft communication officer (Flivo), here of the 7th Panzer Division (note the division emblem under the WL on the nose). The swastika on the nose shows German pilots that these are their own troops. In spite of that, it sometimes happened – especially in the absence of aircraft communication officers – that their own airplanes attacked them.

Right: A 223 in Russia. It has the higher version of the frame antenna. As seen in other pictures, there were also – usually – lower supports. The 223 can be told, by its two lookouts ahead of the driver, from the 261, which had only one. This vehicle carries both a frame antenna and a staff antenna for radio communication.

This vehicle, of Motorcycle Rifle Battalion "GD" of the "Grossdeutschland" Panzer Grenadier Division, is hard to iden-
tify. If it is a 223, it probably would not have a rolled-up tarpaulin ahead of the turret. It may be a 261 on a 222 chassis
(with two lookouts ahead of the driver). (BA)

Light Armored Radio Vehicle, Sd. Kfz. 260 and 261

Strictly speaking, the following vehicles are not armored scout vehicles, as their very name indicates. They were used almost exclusively by the intelligence units of the army. But since they used the same chassis and motors, and almost the same bodies, as the Sd.Kfz. 221, 222 and 223 and are sometimes confused with them, they are portrayed here.

At first they were not armed – only later was a machine gun mounted behind a shield on the 261. Both vehicles lacked a turning turret and usually also lacked a grid over the top opening.

The radio equipment of the 260 included the FuG 7 (for air surveillance units) and FuG Spr.Ger. "a", while the 261 was equipped with the FuG 12 and the FuG Spr.Ger. "a." Externally, the 261 differed from the 260 in having a folding frame antenna. The crew of each vehicle consisted of four men.

In all, 493 of these vehicles were built by Weserhütte and Ritcher between 1940 and 1943.

The two photos below show the Sd.Kfz. 260 (left) and 261. These small armored radio vehicles were based on the chassis of the 221 (later also 222) armored scout vehicle, but always without turret and armament. While the 260 had only a medium-range radio set (staff antenna), the 261 with its frame antenna could communicate at long ranges.

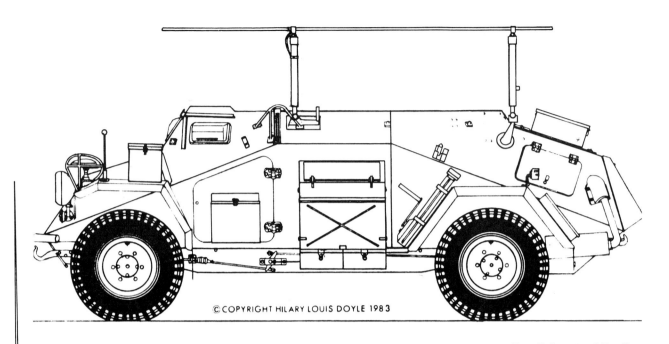

Small Armored Radio
vehicle – Sd.Kfz. 261

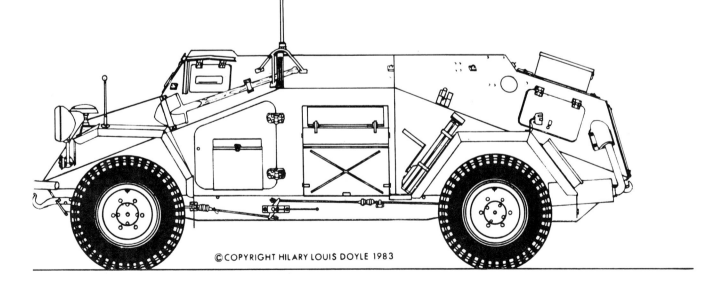

Small Armored Radio
vehicle – Sd.Kfz. 260

Above: a 260 on 222 chassis (two lookouts). The folding screens are easy to see, and the two tool chests on the front deck are worthy of note. (MGFA)

Upper right and right: This is a 261 on 222 chassis. More of these were built than those on the 221 chassis. (BA)

The heavy all-terrain armored personnel carrier (Sd.Kfz. 247) served as a command vehicle for Panzer reconnaissance units (or motorized reconnaissance units). It can be seen in this role on the opposite page, as indicated by the commander's pennant. In the picture above, it serves as a standard-bearer during the big parade in Vienna at the time of Austria's union with the Reich (1938).

Special Motor Vehicles 247 A and B

This was intended as a command vehicle for the staffs of the armored reconnaissance troops. There was an earlier version of it before the war, plus a later one that evolved in wartime. They were designated Types A and B, or Sd.Kfz. 247/1 and 247/2.

The three-axle Type A was built from 1937 to 1939, presumably only ten examples actually being constructed. It was based on the Krupp L2H143 chassis – better known as the chassis of the Krupp Limber – and used the Krupp M 305 horizontally opposed engine, producing 57 HP. The later Type B was built by Daimler-Benz in 1941 and 1942, 58 examples being made. It used the Horch Uniform Chassis II and 3.5 liter Horch motor already used in the 222 and 223. Unlike the armored vehicles previously described, both vehicles had front engines.

The Type A was also used as a standard-bearing vehicle in parades during peacetime. Since the Type B could carry a crew of up to six men, this vehicle can also be regarded as the Wehrmacht's only armored troop transport on wheels. Strictly speaking, both vehicles were small armored scout vehicles, and the three-axle Type A could also be counted among the "heavy" types.

There were two different versions of the 247 (A and B). The older type used the chassis of the Krupp limber and is shown on this page – as a standard-bearer at the left. It weighed 5.2 tons, had a top speed of 70 kph and a range of 350 kilometers.

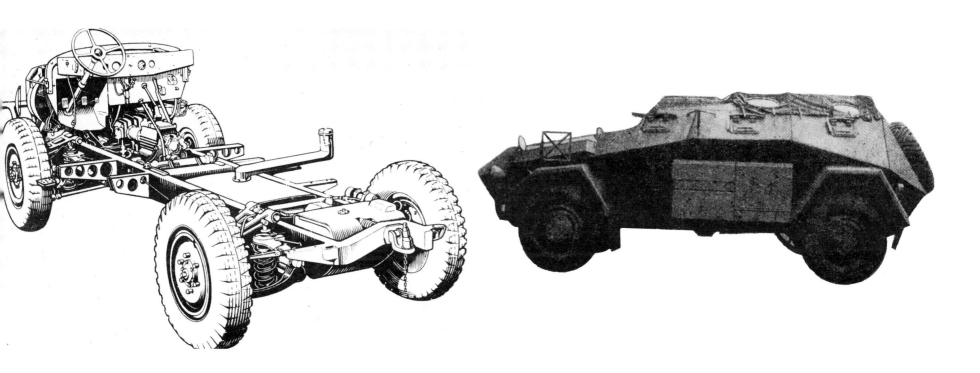

The later 247 had only four wheels and is shown on this page. It was developed during the war.

Above: A drawing of the chassis.

Upper right: In this photo, a somewhat projecting armored air intake can be seen. The later SPW (250 and 251) also show this construction.

Right: The 247 B was used almost exclusively by the Waffen-SS (this vehicle belonged to the "LAH" Panzer Division) and the "Grossdeutschland" Division.

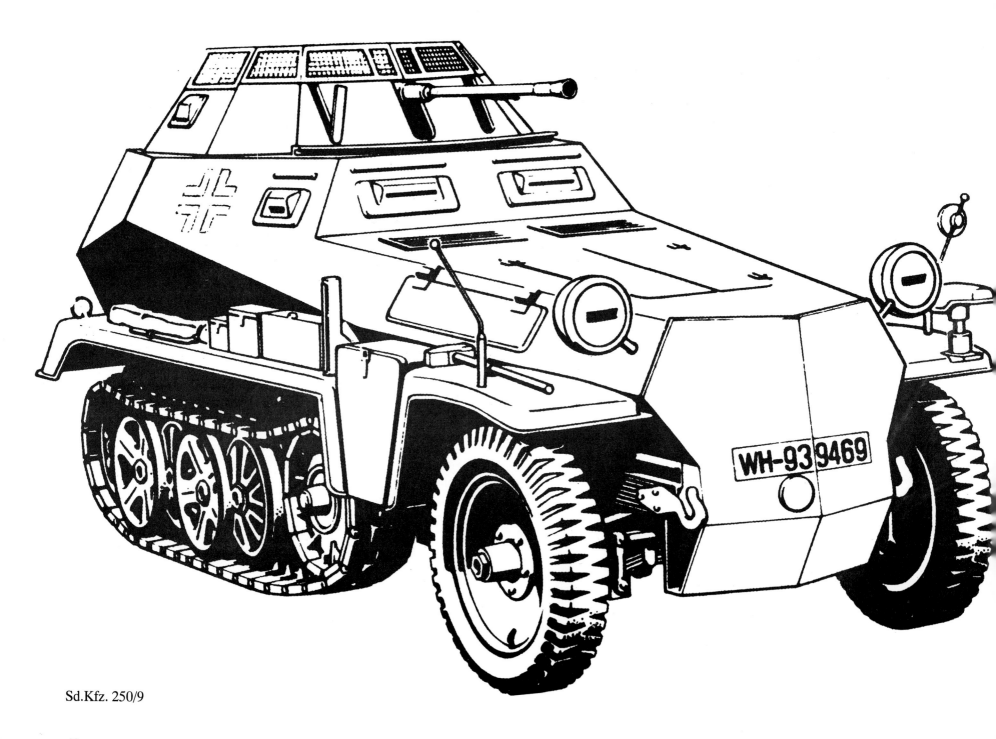

Sd.Kfz. 250/9

Light Scout Vehicle, Sd.Kfz. 250/9 – Caesar

To replace the Type 222 light armored scout vehicle, which was going out of production, the Light Scout vehicle (Sd.Kfz. 250/9) –also called a light Schützenpanzerwagen (2 cm) – was built as of 1943. Arising from the prevailing problems of the time (few good roads and much mud) of the Russian terrain, this was the first step in the wrong direction, to tracked vehicles (too loud, too slow, too heavy, too little performance, too vulnerable for use by combat troops) for the reconnaissance units.

There were too different types of it, depending on whether the earlier Schützenpanzer version with angled sidewalls or the later type with straight walls was used. Usually the earlier type used the earlier reconnaissance turret, while the later type had the turret with the hanging gun mount and higher grids.

The crew consisted of three men, the weight was six tons, and the FuG 12 radio equipment was installed.

Below: Three light scout vehicles on the steppes of southern Russia in 1943.

The two pictures above show the "Caesar" at left in its older form with short armor plate, and at right in its new form with vertical or filled-out sidewalls. The latter had the newer turret with hanging mount. This was occasionally installed in the older version as well. The photo at left shows that mounting the armored reconnaissance turret on a somewhat modified chassis of the Skoda 38 (t) tank was also considered. (1 x BA)

Opposite page: A 250 captured and utilized by the Americans (thus the emblems on the armor plate) is shown here. It is the older version, but includes a hanging gun mount.

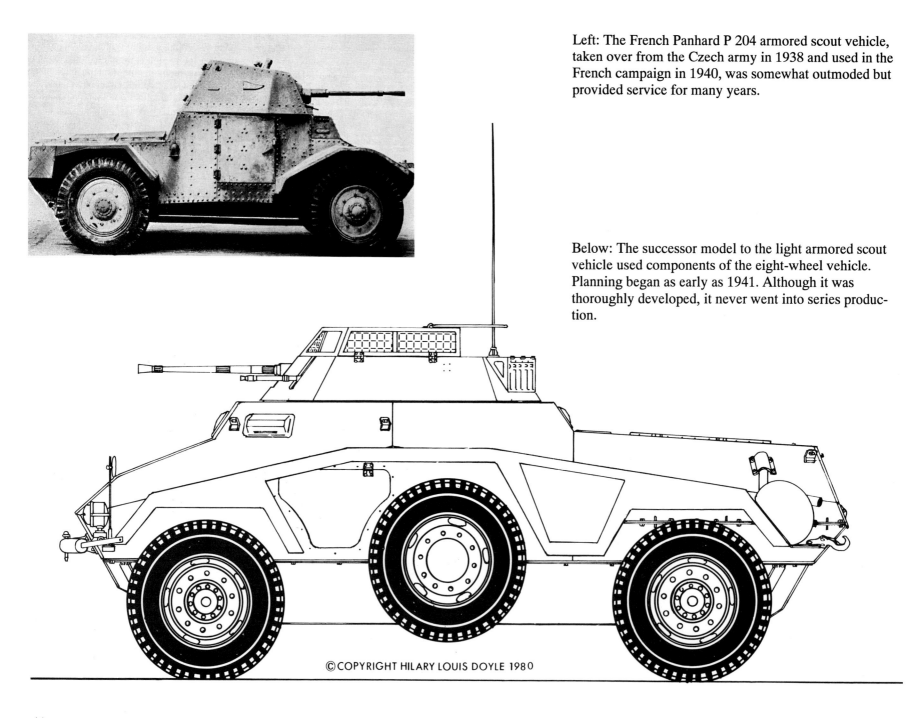

Left: The French Panhard P 204 armored scout vehicle, taken over from the Czech army in 1938 and used in the French campaign in 1940, was somewhat outmoded but provided service for many years.

Below: The successor model to the light armored scout vehicle used components of the eight-wheel vehicle. Planning began as early as 1941. Although it was thoroughly developed, it never went into series production.

©COPYRIGHT HILARY LOUIS DOYLE 1980

Panhard Armored Scout Vehicle 178-P 204 (f)

This light French scout vehicle was taken over by the Wehrmacht, Waffen-SS and police in great numbers after the occupation of Czechoslovakia in 1939 and the French campaign of 1940. The following versions of it existed, resulting in part from German revisions:

– Gun vehicle with French 2.5 cm Pak gun
– Gun vehicle with German 5 cm Pak gun
– Machine-gun vehicle with French machine gun

– Radio vehicle with German bow antenna
– Armored rail vehicle, usually armed with the French 2.5 cm Pak and German bow antenna.

It carried a four-man crew, its top speed was 72 kph, and its range on the road was 300 kilometers. With a weight of 8.5 tons, it was the heaviest scout vehicle used by the Germans. All in all, it was a good vehicle. It is worth noting that it saw service on both sides during the French campaign, since vehicles taken over from the Czech army were already in German service in 1940.

Below: Two interesting versions of this vehicle. At left, with German bow antenna, and at right, as a railway tank in Russia. (2 x BA)

The Panhards taken over from the Czech army were already put to use in the French campaign (for example, by the motorized reconnaissance regiment of the 7th Panzer Division). In this campaign, this scout vehicle was used by both sides. (BA)

Above: Its widest use was by the SS police divisions for action against partisans.

Left: Here is a version with a German 3.7 cm gun. These reached the troops only in limited numbers. (BA)

Technical Data

KFZ 13 and 14

Motor	Adler "Standard 6"
Cylinders	6 in-line
Bore x stroke	75 x 110 mm
Displacement	2916 cc
Compression ratio	5.3 : 1
RPM normal/maximum	3000/3200 RPM
Performance	51/60 HP
Power to weight	27 HP/ton
Valves	Side valves
Bearings	7 journal
Carburetor	1 Pallas SAD 3
Firing order	1-5-3-6-2-4
Starter	Bosch AJ 0.8/6
Generator	Bosch RJVC 90/6-1100
Battery	1 6-volt
Fuel pump	Low-pressure
Cooling	Water
Clutch	Dry single-plate
Gearbox	Shear [Vorgelege]
Speeds	4 forward, 1 reverse
Drive wheels	Rear
Axle ratio	1 : 6.1
Top speed	45-50 kph on, 25-30 kph off road
Range	240 km on, 150 km off road
Front suspension	Rigid axle
Steering	Worm-gear
Turning circle	15.0 meters
Springs	Semi-elliptic longitudinal leaf
Lubrication	Bowen central
Brake system	ATE-Lockheed
Operation	Hydraulic
Type	Inside drum
Foot brake affects	Four wheels
Hand brake affects	Gearbox
Wheel type	Sheet steel
Tire size	600-20
Front/rear track	1440 mm
Wheelbase	2840 mm
Ground clearance	210 mm
Overall length	4200 mm
Overall width	1700 mm
Overall height	1500 mm
Chassis weight	1100 kp
Max. gross weight	2200 (2250) kp
Load limit	350 kp
Seats	3
Fuel consumption	18 liters, 25 off road/100 km
Oil consumption	0.6 liters/100 km
Fuel capacity	70 liters
Armor plate	8 mm all around
Climbing ability	15 degrees
Wading ability	500 mm
Armament	1 MG 13

LIGHT ARMORED SCOUT vehicle SD.KFZ. 222

Motor	AU/Horch 3.5 liter (3.8 liter)
Cylinders	V-8, 66 degrees
Bore x stroke	78 x 92 mm
Displacement	3517 cc
Compression ratio	6.3 : 1
Engine speed	3600 RPM
Performance	75 HP
Power to weight	15.62 HP/ton
Valves	Dropped
Bearings	5 journal
Carburetor	1 Solex 32 JPF
Firing order	1-8-3-6-4-5-2-7
Starter	Bosch BJH 1.4/12 RS 6-46
Generator	Bosch RKC 130/12-825, etc.
Batteries	2 12-volt Ah
Fuel pump	Solex
Cooling	Water
Clutch	Single-disc F & S PF 20 KZM
Gearbox	AU/Horch uniform shear
Speeds	5 forward, 1 reverse
Drive wheels	All four
Axle ratio	1 : 6.375
Top speed	80 (90) kph
Range	350 km
Front suspension	Independent
Steering	ZF Ross worm-gear
Turning circle	A = 10, V = 17 meters
Springs	Coil
Lubrication	Vogel central
Brake system	AU/Horch
Brake effect	Mechanical (hydraulic)
Brake type	Inside drum
Foot brake affects	4 wheels
Hand brake affects	4 wheels
Wheel type	Sheet steel
Tire size	210-18 all-terrain
Track front/rear	1610 (1646) mm
Wheelbase	2800 mm
Ground clearance	260 mm
Overall length	4800 mm
Overall width	1950 mm
Overall height	2000 mm
Firing height	1750 mm
Chassis weight	1960 kp
Max. gross weight	4800 kp
Load limit	600 kp
Seats	3
Fuel consumption	28.8 liters/100 km
Oil consumption	0.2 liters/100 km
Fuel capacity	50 + 50 = 100 liters
Armor: hull front	14.5, later 30 mm
sides & rear	8 mm
turret front	14.5 mm
sides & rear	8 mm
Climbing ability	20 degrees
Climbing distance	250 mm
Wading ability	600 mm
Armament	1 2 cm KwK 30/38 (180) & 1 MG 34 1050)

LIGHT ARMORED RADIO VEHICLE SD.KFZ. 261

Motor	AU/Horch 3.8 liter
Cylinders	V-8, 66 degrees
Bore x stroke	78 x 100 mm
Displacement	3823 cc
Compression ratio	6.1 : 1
Engine speed	3600 RPM
Performance	90 HP
Power to weight	17.04 HP/ton
Valves	Dropped
Bearings	5 journal
Carburetors	2 Solex 30 BFLH
Firing order	1-8-3-6-4-5-2-7
Starter	Bosch EJD 1.8/12
Generator	Bosch RKCN 130/12-825
Battery	1 12 volt 75 Ah
Fuel pumps	2 Solex
Cooling	Water
Clutch	F & S H 32 single-plate
Gearbox	AU/Horch Uniform shear
Speeds	5 forward, 1 reverse
Drive wheels	All four
Axle ratio	1 : 6.375
Top speed	85 kph
Range	310 km on, 200 km off road
Front suspension	Independent
Steering	ZF Ross worm-gear four-wheel
Turning circle	15.0/9.5 meters
Springs	Coil
Lubrication	Vogel central
Brake system	A. Teves
Brake effect	Hydraulic
Brake type	Inner drum
Foot brake affects	4 wheels
Hand brake affects	4 wheels
Wheel type	Sheet steel
Tire size	210-18 all-terrain
Track, front/rear	1646 mm
Wheelbase	2800 mm
Ground clearance	255 mm
Overall length	4830 mm
Overall width	1990 mm
Overall height	1780 mm
Chassis weight	2000 kp
Max. gross weight	4300 kp
Load limit	600 kp
Seats	4
Fuel consumption	28.2 liters/100 km
Oil consumption	0.2 liters/100 km
Fuel capacity	100 liters in 2 tanks
Armor: hull front	30 mm
rear slope	8 mm
Climbing ability	22 degrees
Climbing distance	250 mm
Wading ability	600 mm
Armament	1 MP (192)

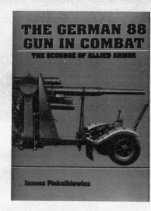

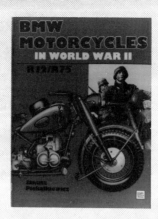

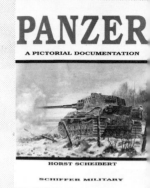